THE
FOOTBALL
BOOK

A QUIZ BOOK
FACT BOOK
PUZZLE BOOK

Matt Maguire

Also from Candescent Press

Publisher Information

Candescent Press

info@candescentpress.co.uk

www.candescentpress.co.uk

Copyright © 2016 Matt Maguire and Candescent Press.

This book is an unofficial publication and is not authorised in any way by any of the football clubs mentioned. The information is vaguely accurate – but who knows these days? If you find something that is so wrong it makes your blood boil more than an incorrectly given penalty in the 87th minute, then send us a message!

Welcome to The Football Book.

We had a lot of fun putting together this book so we really hope you enjoy it too.

Given that the book is full of light hearted mockery, and tales of games which inevitably involved losers, we're bound to have offended your team or country somewhere. If we haven't, we're very sorry and will try and rectify it when we write a sequel.

The writers are based in England so when we refer to The Premier League or the top division we mean the English ones. Sorry Scotland and Wales, and the rest of the world (but you are included too!)

Pat yourself on the back!

We donate a large part of our profits on each book to charity – so thanks for buying the book (or go and give the person who bought it a big hug!)

So far we've helped charities working in the areas of Mental Health, Homelessness, Dementia and more. We'll keep going till people stop buying our books, so if you liked the book and want to help, a review would be appreciated!

Contents

THE FOOTBALL BOOK

A QUIZ BOOK
FACT BOOK
PUZZLE BOOK

Name the Team #1

Find the answer at the bottom of the next page.

Unusual Injuries:
The TV Remote

#1 Robbie Keane

Robbie Keane – He's won so many caps for Ireland that, if they were actual caps (and they used to be, so no sniggering!), he could dress up over 100 dogs in an amusing way, and still have lots left over to play "toss the cap onto the stick."*

Still – being a brilliant Irish footballer doesn't mean you can't cause yourself a major injury when trying to change the TV channel. Robbie managed to rupture his knee cartilage when he stretched to grab the remote control in 1998.

"Is ait an mac an saol" as we're told they might say in Ireland.

*this is a game that I think we've just made up.

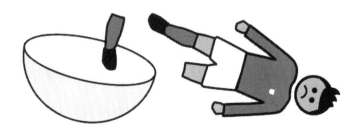

Name the Team #1: Burnley (Burn (Bruce) Lee)

QUIZ 1 – Back in Training

1. Which club's fans sing *Delilah*, the song made famous by Tom Jones?

2. The always entertaining ex-Manchester United star Eric Cantona played himself in which Ken Loach film?

3. Which team won the very first European Cup?

4. Which eccentric manager said, after winning a match, "I couldn't be more chuffed if I were a badger at the start of the mating season"?

5. Which team won the FA Cup an impressive four seasons in a row in the 1880s? Bury, Bolton or Blackburn Rovers?

6. Three players were sent off at the 1978 World Cup Finals. Two were from which East European country?

7. Whose autobiography was called *Crossing the Line*?

8. Which West Midlands club won the very first English League Cup in 1961?

9. Manchester United won the first Premier League title, but which team won the final First Division title the previous year?

10. Which team is also known as the Addicks?

See page 72 for the answers.

We'll just have to do this another time

Going out with a bang!

A match in Sweden between IFK Gothenburg and Malmo was abandoned in 2016 when a firework was thrown at one of the subs. Tobias Sana of Malmo was warming up when a firework went off by his feet. Now, the ref would probably take a dim view of this, but it's what happened next that caused the abandonment of the match. Sana, walked over to the corner flag, picked it up, and launched it into the crowd, full on javelin style! He might have been facing a ban from the football authorities, but we wouldn't be surprised if the Swedish Olympic javelin team aren't on the phone too!

9, 8, 7 … and we're off!

If you think non-league football can't be exciting, then you've never watched a match in Division Five South of the Almary Green Anglian Combination. Admittedly the quality isn't quite up there with Division Four of the Almary Green Anglian Combination, but there's a video of a particular game between East Harling Reserves and Corton Seltic that's worth checking out. Corton Seltic were up against it from the start, having begun the game with only nine men (you're right – this probably would not happen in the Champion's League) – but from almost the first attack of the match, one of their players committed a professional foul, and was sent off. A second player was then sent off for abusing the referee (probably complaining about only having 8 players left!) A couple more players walked off in disgust, before a quick thinking East Harling player took advantage of the confusion and curled a beauty into the top corner. Sadly, probably the best goal he'll ever score won't count, as the rest of the Seltic players walked off, and the match was abandoned.

The Last Post

Chester and Plymouth Argyle met in the first leg of a League Cup match in 1981, when disaster struck*. The game was level after 85 minutes, and Plymouth were probably thinking it was a job well done, with the home leg still to come … until Chester keeper Grenville Millington intervened. Diving to make a save, he collided with the post, which promptly broke. It couldn't be fixed, and no spare was available, so the game was called off. Unlucky Plymouth had to make another 500 mile round trip a week later – but they secured another draw, and won the return leg, so all that travel wasn't completely wasted. Unfortunately, they did get knocked out in the next round by Middlesbrough, a return journey of nearly 800 miles!

*ok, not quite a disaster, but certainly mild inconvenience.

A quick one?

St Austell and Bodmin Town. Abandoned after 58 seconds. Fog. Ref Neil Hunniset said, "I wanted to see if the fog would clear."

Who's the player?

1. He was born on 25th April 1947, and is a three time winner of the Ballon D'or. He played in the United States, with the Los Angeles Aztecs and the Washington Diplomats, and went on to manage the Catalonia 'national' team. Name that player.

2. Born on the 29th September 1976, he began and ended his professional career at Dynamo Kyiv. He also played over 100 times for his national team, scoring almost 50 goals. Who's the player?

3. Born in Rosario on the 24th June 1987, he was a youth player with Newell's Old Boys, and later won an Olympic gold medal for his country. Who is he?

4. She began her senior career with Vasco de Gama in Brazil, and was the FIFA World Player of the Year five times. Name the player?

5. Born in Chester on the 14th December 1979, this footballer ended his playing career with Stoke City. He also scored four goals for England at World Cup finals. Name the player.

See page 100 for the answers.

QUIZ 2 – Pre-Season Friendlies

1. English clubs won the European Cup every year between 1977 and 1982. Can you name the teams who won during that time? Double points if you get the order right!

2. Which team is also known as the Baggies?

3. Only one Leicester City player scored a league hat-trick during their 2015/16 title winning campaign? Name that player.

4. Which club, who play their home matches at Gigg Lane, won the first FA Cup of the 20th Century?

5. Which club played home games at the Britannia Stadium?

6. Which European country was the first to host a World Cup?

7. Which ex-England manager once said, "I was just saying to your colleague, the referee has got me the sack, thank him ever so much for that, won't you?"

8. Which London based team won the first three English Women's League Cup finals?

9. In what year did Luis Suárez win the Ballon d'Or?

10. By what name are the fans of the Scottish national team widely known?

See page 74 for the answers.

Name the Trophy #1

Someone has made you sit in a chair, and is holding up pieces of black card in the shape of football trophies from across the world. We don't know why they're doing this, but we do know that you'd better get the answers right!

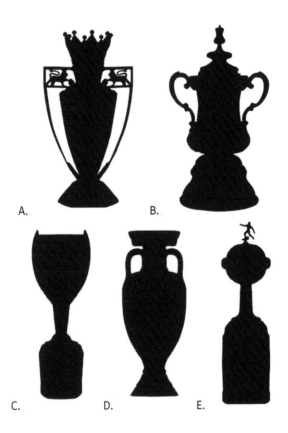

A.

B.

C.

D.

E.

Answers on page 103.

Mixed up Stadiums – Anagrams #1

We've mixed up the letters in the names of some famous (and not so famous) football stadiums. Can you work them out?

An extra point for naming the team that played at each stadium.

1. rat lord doff

2. I am goldfish tut

3. poor kings ado

4. hit hat renewal

5. mistaking row dupe

6. Cat convert age

7. Ancient ad

8. A pork owed

9. A roar crowd

You can find the answers on page 107

Big Money transfers!
What would you do?

#1 Kaká

In an alternate universe, Real Madrid decide not to buy Kaká.

Instead they spend the money driving him around the entire Brazilian border in a taxi 4269 times.

Name the Team #2

Find the answer at the bottom of the next page.

QUIZ 3 - The Season Kicks Off

1. Which country's teams have won the UEFA Women's Champions League (also known as the UEFA Women's Cup) more than any other?

2. Whose autobiography was called *Full Time*?

3. 'Blue is the colour' is sung by fans of which Premier League club?

4. Which manager said, "I wouldn't say I was the best manager in the business, but I was in the top one"?

5. Which team is also known as the Bantams?

6. In 2002, two countries hosted the World Cup Finals for the first time. Can you name them?

7. Who were the first sponsors of the Premier League?

8. Kevin Keegan is the only English player to have won more than one Ballon d'Or. He won both times while playing for the same team - can you name the club?

9. In which decade did Aston Villa win their first FA Cup?

10. Which club played home games at the King Power Stadium?

See page 76 for the answers.

Name the Team #2: Swansea (Swan C)

Name the Team #3

Find the answer at the bottom of the next page.

Extra! Extra! Read all about it!

How many halves does a football match have? If you just answered, "Two, of course. You muppet! Who do you think I am? I know the rules," then we've got news for you - sometimes it's three! Ok, by sometimes we mean one time, but here's how the story goes …

The year is 1894, it was the first day of the season and Derby had travelled to Sunderland for their opening match. All the players were ready, laces tied, Mozart on the gramophone (or whatever it is players did before the invention of Beats headphones), but no referee in sight. The man in black, Mr Kirkham (we don't think they had first names in the 19th Century) had missed his train, and had to send a telegram stating that he might not make the match. A replacement was found, and a Mr Conqueror took to the pitch instead, whistle in hand, ready to officiate, firmly but fairly.

Roll on half time, and Derby were already 3-0 down, when who should arrive, but the originally appointed arbiter of fair play, Mr Kirkham. Now, rules are rules, and sometimes you just have to show a replacement official who's the boss, so Mr Kirkham stepped in, twirled his impeccably waxed moustache (please note, some details are embroidered for your reading pleasure), and offered Derby the chance to start the match again.

Which of course they took. Fast forward 45 minutes, and in a depressing case of déjà vu for the Rams fans, Derby were again 3-0 down. The 'third half' saw Sunderland score another five goals, and Derby went home with no points, having conceded eleven times in just over two hours and fifteen minutes.

Three is the magic number

I'm sure many of you remember Graham Poll finding that little bit extra at the 2006 World Cup, but the story deserves telling again. In a crucial group stage decider, Croatia needed to beat Australia to reach the second round. In a delightfully entertaining last 15 minutes, Harry Kewell scored a late equaliser to level the match at 2-2, putting the Socceroos into the next round. However, keen to make his own impact on the game, referee Poll managed to create a little history by giving Josip Simunic three yellow cards. In the last ten minutes Poll sent off two players (one from each side), and should have sent off Simunic, after giving him a second yellow in the final minute of the game. In the spirit of fair play, Simunic sort of put things right by getting into an argument with the referee after the final whistle, getting a further yellow card, and finally getting his marching orders. Graham Poll "retired" from refereeing international games following the match.

You Called Your Stadium What? #1

These days stadiums can have some pretty silly names. Apparently history means nothing when some company with a dodgy name wants to pay a few hundred quid to stick their name on your club's stadium. We've found some of the most ridiculous and matched them up with ones we made up – Which is the real stadium?

1. Point of Sale Park or Cashpoint Arena?

2. Hunky Dorys Park or Okey Dokey Stadium?

3. Tony Macaroni Arena or Campo Carbonara?

4. Burger King Stadium or Pizza Hut Park?

5. The Lard Pan or The Dripping Pan?

6. Middelfart Stadium or Upperguff Arena?

7. Snickers Bay Park or Kitkat Crescent?

8. Cash Converters Arena or Bargain Booze Stadium?

See page 104 for the answers.

QUIZ 4 – The First Round of The Cup

1. Who won the PFA Players' Player of the Year in 1994?

2. Who hosted the first World Cup Finals in 1930?

3. Which club played home games at Vicarage Road?

4. Which club's fans sing 'I'm Forever Blowing Bubbles'?

5. In 2003, Milan beat Juventus to win the European Cup at which English team's ground?

6. We've all heard of Match of the Day, but from 2001-2004 the BBC lost the rights to broadcast Premier League highlights to ITV. What was ITV's highlights show called?

7. Which Scottish team won the 1983 European Cup Winners' Cup?

8. Which manager (who had a pretty impressive career as a player too) called his autobiography *Walking on Water*?

9. Which sister and brother have represented the English and Nigerian national teams, respectively?

10. Which manager said, "Mind you, I've been here during the bad times too - one year we came second"?

See page 78 for the answers.

He can play a bit, that lad!
A Messi Spot the Difference!

There are nine differences between the pictures on this page and the next – find them all, and give yourself an extra present!

He can play a bit, that lad!
A Messi Spot the Difference!

See page 102 for the answers.

Very, very naughty or very, very silly

The fastest red card

Within seconds of the start of a match, a crunching tackle is made. The referee walks over and produces a red card – sent off within thirty seconds! What drama!

Lee Todd would laugh at this point, "Thirty seconds? What took so long? How about just two?" That's right, in an October 2000 Sunday league game, Cross Farm Park Celtic striker Lee Todd was sent off after just TWO SECONDS. Todd, facing away from the referee, was surprised when the whistle blew to start the match. "F*** me, that was loud," he said, not to anyone in particular. The ref, clearly not a fan of bad language, immediately sent him off.

Or maybe this one's faster?

In 2007, Keith Gillespie came onto the pitch as a sub, and was sent off before the game restarted. He'd been on the pitch just over 10 seconds, but for ZERO seconds of actual play.

Gillespie, playing for Sheffield United at the time, came onto the pitch with his team already two goals down to Reading. Within seconds he'd clashed with Stephen Hunt, elbowing him in the face. Referee, Mark Halsey, had no choice but to send him straight back off the pitch!

Silly boys

Sometimes players get in a bit of a tizz during a match, and start punching each other. It's not big, it's not clever, but at least it's usually players from opposing teams. Not so in March 2005, when Lee Bowyer and Kieron Dyer, both playing for Newcastle United at the time, decided that simply losing to Aston villa wasn't enough to ruin their manager's day, so they decided to have a fight. Both players were quickly sent off.

According to Dyer, they fell out because he wasn't passing to Bowyer, and when asked why, he told his colleague it was because he was rubbish! Dyer also said he didn't realise you could be sent off for having a fight with someone on your own side, and was genuinely surprised the ref just didn't let them get on with it.

Is it a goal? Is it a save?
No, it's Oliver Khan – Superbizzarogoalkeeperman!

Now Oliver Khan was a pretty good goalkeeper. He won the Champions League, a European Championship and a bundle of Bundesliga titles. But he was also a little bit unpredictable.

Our favourite moment happened in the last minute of a match against Hansa Rostock. Playing for Bayern, and 3-2 down, he ran up the pitch for a last minute corner. Would he score? Would he be the hero? Well ... the ball ended up in the net ... and Khan put it there. Unfortunately he flat out punched it. Thump! Straight into the goal. Clear as day.

Kahn was sent off, and Bayern lost the match. Numpty!

Unusual Injuries:
The Warning Sign

#2 Richard Wright

Richard Wright has FA Cup and Premier League winner's medals from his time with Arsenal … and he even played for England. He also broke some kind of record at Manchester City, where he managed four seasons without ever actually playing. Not bad for an international footballer (albeit one who give away two penalties on his England debut!). Sadly it wasn't all highs for Richard, as he once injured himself when he dived during training and landed on a wooden sign.

The sign said "Don't train in this area".

QUIZ 5 - The Early Leaders

1. In 1986, Steaua Bucharest became the first Eastern European club to win the European Cup. Which country are they from?

2. In 2010, the 'Europe only' Ballon d'Or combined with FIFA's World Player of the Year to become an award for the best player anywhere in the world. Who won that 2010 award?

3. Who coined the phrase "squeaky-bum time" – for when the season is nearing its denouement?

4. Arsenal won the UEFA Women's Cup in 2006/07. In the final, they beat a team from which country?

5. Which ex-Premier League player turned TV Pundit called his biography *Killa*?

6. Which team is also known as the Black Cats?

7. The ground is the Liberty Stadium but who are the team?

8. Which brand were the very first sponsors of the English Football League?

9. "Glory Glory ..." – if we sang the rest, you'd know the answer. Which club's song is this?

10. Who won the FA Cup in 1971?

See page 80 for the answers.

Match the Club to the Country

All of these teams have played in the Champions League (ok, they didn't reach the final, but qualifying still counts, right?) Anyway – can you match the club to the country they play in?

Lincoln Red Imps	**Andorra**
Pyunik	**Armenia**
FC Santa Coloma	**Estonia**
Folgore	**Faroe Islands**
The New Saints	**Northern Ireland**
Levadia Tallinn	**Iceland**
B36 Tórshavn	**Montenegro**
Crusaders	**Gibraltar**
Rudar Pljevlja	**San Marino**
Stjarnan	**Wales**

You'll find the answers on page 114.

Name the Team #4

Find the answer at the bottom of the next page.

1966 and All That!

In 1966 England won the World Cup. We don't like to talk about it, so it's probably news to you – but now you know, why not try to find the names of the winning team in the word search below. When you find them, it'll be like winning all over again.

```
N N U G O R D O N B A N K S S
O S O V N P B A U L L S O R T
B T X T L O D B L K E S E C N
B N G X L X S A F Y S T S A U
Y O U E J R B L G F E F B Q H
S T D P O N A C I P B O X L R
T L G M A R A H N W B E D A E
I R G L H Q G I C B Y D F U G
L A A M C F T E Y Y M A N O O
E H H B O R M M C Q B U R F R
S C H D A Y O F F O B B I S Y
J K A M D O P W H B H T O X B
L C W C R G A Y L P D E M B R
S A M E L W H P U D R Z N C W
P J T S R U H F F O E G C L Z
```

GORDON BANKS, GEORGE COHEN, JACK CHARLTON, BOBBY MOORE, RAY WILSON, NOBBY STILES, ALAN BALL, BOBBY CHARLTON, MARTIN PETERS, GEOFF HURST, ROGER HUNT

You can find the solution on page 115.

QUIZ 6 - The Local Derby

1. Who won the World Cup final in 2006?

2. The ground is Brunton Park but who are the team?

3. Which whisky brand were the first sponsor of the Scottish League Cup?

4. Everton run onto the pitch to the theme from which 1960s TV police show?

5. In what year did Luis Suarez win the PFA Players' Player of the Year award?

6. Which club have won the European Cup and its successor, The Champions League, the most times?

7. Whose autobiography is called *My Turn*?

8. Who won the FA Cup in 1981?

9. 2015/16 was the first time Leicester City had won England's top division. They joined an exclusive club of only five 'one-time winners' - can you name the other four?

10. Who was the first player to reach 150 caps for the England Women's team?

See page 82 for the answers.

Big Money transfers!
What would you do?

#2 David Luiz

David Luiz divides opinions like no other player. When he's on form he can look like a majestic lion playing against quivering antelope. Yet, when Germany were thrashing Brazil in the World Cup 7-1, he decided the best way to stop the Germans scoring was to create a new position on the pitch: the winger-striker-attacking-defensive-midfield-centre back (The WSADMCB for short). So, our question to Mr Paris St Germain is: Why take the chance and buy David Luiz, when you could get 5,000,000 Sideshow Bob talking toy figures instead?

Who Stole The Cup?

The most famous 'stolen' cup story is of course the tale of the 1996 World Cup. It was stolen before the tournament in England, and there was even a ransom note.

The police set up a sting to catch the thief, but the man they caught denied stealing the cup himself, wouldn't tell them where it might be, and simply said he was acting on behalf of a mysterious man known only as "The Pole".

Fortunately, the Police weren't the only ones on the 'scent' of the cup. A week after it went missing, a dog called Pickles was sniffing around a hedge near his home (being a dog that's pretty much standard behaviour), when he discovered a parcel. It only turned out to be the lost cup, and Pickles became a national celebrity! But the World Cup wasn't the only trophy that ever went missing, as Aston Villa know only too well ...

Aston Villains?

In 1895, the FA Cup was stolen when it was in the possession of Aston Villa – and to make matters worse Villa also lost a European Cup!

The FA Cup was stolen while on display in a Birmingham shop window, following Villa's 1-0 win over local rivals West Bromwich

Albion. A £10 reward was offered, but the cup was never recovered, and the FA even fined Villa £25 for losing it.

Nothing more was heard for over sixty years until, in 1958, an 80-year-old called Harry Burge owned up. He claimed, in an interview with a national newspaper, that he and two other rogues had stolen the cup, and melted it down to make dodgy coins!

His story didn't quite match the original case notes, so there are still doubts about whether he was the culprit who half-inched the trophy. Still, try asking your own 80-year-old Grandad what he was doing on a Wednesday night 63 years ago, and you might not get an accurate account either. What isn't in doubt is that it wasn't the last time Villa were careless with a cup …

Roll on 1982, and Aston Villa were champions of Europe (that might be the most unbelievable part of the story, but it's definitely true!) Now, this was a different era, one which apparently pre-dates 'common sense', and so the players were allowed to take one of the most valuable trophies in the world with them to the pub – and, one night in the Fox Inn, the cup went missing while Villa players Gordon Cowans and Colin Gibson were having a game of darts.

The West Midlands police were put on full alert trying to track down the cup, but bizarrely it turned up in a Sheffield police station later that night. Rather than arrest the man who brought in the cup, the police quickly got two teams together and, in full uniform, played a match in the middle of the night. The winners got to hold the trophy aloft, and had their photo taken, before it was returned to Villa the next day.

They Started Out Where?

All the players below have represented England, and play for some of the biggest teams in the world – but can you name the clubs where they made their professional debuts?

1. Joe Hart

2. Dele Alli

3. Wayne Rooney

4. Eric Dier

5. Gary Cahill

6. John Stones

7. Daniel Sturridge

8. Alex Oxlade-Chamberlain

9. Jordan Henderson

10. Fraser Forster

See page 107 for the answers.

Name the Trophy #2

More trophy silhouettes – This time they're in a dark room and being held behind a white sheet with a torch shining on them. For you, the challenge is the same – name the Football trophies from around the world!

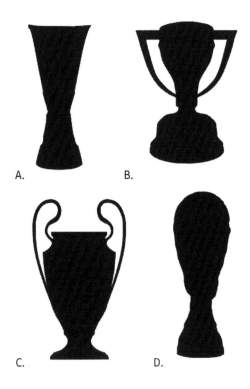

A.

B.

C.

D.

See page 110 for the answers.

Name the Team #5

Find the answer at the bottom of the next page.

QUIZ 7 - The Busy Xmas Period

1. Who won the FA Cup in 1984?

2. The 1970 World Cup finals were hosted by Mexico, but which country won the competition?

3. Which London club are known as the Hoops?

4. How many times was Gareth Bale voted the PFA Players' Player of the Year?

5. Which manager said of his club's fans, "If you eat caviar every day it's difficult to return to sausages"?

6. When Celtic were beaten by Inverness Caledonian Thistle, in February 2000, what was the famous headline in the next day's paper?

7. Which ex-player wrote the book *How Not to Be a Professional Footballer*?

8. Which team is also known as the Canaries?

9. One of England's most successful women's teams was founded in 1969 by lottery ticket sellers at the Belle View stadium. In which town were the 'Belles' based?

10. The ground is Ashton Gate Stadium but who are the team?

You can find the answers on page 84.

Mixed up Teams – Anagrams #2

We've mixed up the letters in the names of some football clubs. Can you work them out?

1.   Earl Bacon

2.   Bar Witch Snowmobile

3.   A Twitching Ale

4.   Phantoms Out

5.   Vital Loans

6.   I Select Unwanted

7.   Square Prank Genres

8.   Ruby

9.   Lawn Fit Hoax

You can find the answers on page 111.

Football at War

Now we all get a little bit worked up about football occasionally, but I'm pretty sure none of us would start a war because of it. That wasn't the case in El Salvador and Honduras, where the Soccer War was fought in 1969. La Guerra del Fútbol (as they say in Spanish speaking Honduras and El Salvador*) had been brewing for a while, with economic problems and migration between the two countries causing tension, particularly near their shared border. Both countries had similar populations, but Honduras is much larger, so unsurprisingly many Salvadorans had moved to Honduras to work. With the situation already volatile, over the course of three tempestuous World Cup qualifying matches, anger spilled over into violence.

The final match, a deciding play-off, took place on 26th June, and El Salvador were victorious. Later that same day, diplomatic relations between the two countries were broken off (a fancy way of saying the two governments stopped talking to each other!), and, following a couple of weeks of rising tensions, on the 14th July, El Salvador invaded Honduras. Within days, both countries were suffering, and the Organization of American States (OAS) was able to negotiate a ceasefire. The war had lasted just 100 hours, but sadly thousands of lives had already been lost.

*notice how we changed the order of the names? We want to be even handed here, and frankly don't want to be blamed if things kick off again in the future.

The Football Battalion

During the First World War, an infantry battalion was formed by the British Army with numerous professional footballers as its core. Players from just about every corner of the country joined up, and fought in some of the bloodiest battles of the war. Walter Tull, playing for Northampton Town at the time of his call up, became the very first black officer in the British army (despite the fact that some astonishingly racist military rules at the time actually banned black people from becoming officers). Sadly he died in battle in 1918.

A memorial for Walter was unveiled at Northampton's Sixfield Stadium in 1999.

DANGER! Unexploded football pitch!

The Second World War could have had a huge impact on the amateur footballers of Portland, in Dorset. For fifty years, Portland United had been playing with an unexploded bomb inches beneath the surface of their pitch. It was only in 1995, not long after a quarrying firm had taken over the land, that the device was discovered. 4000 people had to be evacuated while it was defused, but with five decades of studded boots trampling just inches away, it could have been much worse!

QUIZ 8 - Mid-Season Madness!

1. Who won the Scottish Football League Premier Division in the 1982/83 season?

2. Who won the World Cup final in 1982?

3. By what nickname are Stoke City known?

4. How many times have the host country won the World Cup? If you can name them all, give yourself ten imaginary bonus points!

5. Which Midlands side won the English First Division title three times in the 1950s?

6. Which London Women's Super League team did England winger Karen Carney sign for in December 2015?

7. Which English manager has won the European Cup/ Champions League the most times?

8. The ground is Roots Hall but who are the team?

9. Which Italian manager, who never played top level football, said, "You don't have to have been a horse to be a jockey."?

10. Who won the FA Cup in 2008?

See page 86 for the answers.

Big Money transfers!
What would you do?

#4 Ronaldo

Ronaldo signed a six-year contract with Real Madrid in 2009. Over the next six years he only won La Liga once, while Barcelona won it four times! Now, Ronaldo has been banging in 60 goals a season, so it's not been all that bad for him. Still, if anyone at Real Madrid was jealous, they could take a tour of Barcelona's Camp Nou stadium and look at the trophy whenever they wanted. In fact, for the same price as Ronaldo, the entire population of Madrid could take the tour, and they'd still have 10 Euros each to spend on souvenirs.

Match the Manager to the Club

Can you match these famous managers to the clubs they first managed?

Bobby Robson	Campania Puteolana
Alex Ferguson	Benfica
Fabio Capello	East Stirlingshire
Claudio Ranieri	Dunfermline
Brian Clough	Fulham
Sven-Göran Eriksson	Reggiana
José Mourinho	Hartlepool United
Carlo Ancelotti	Milan
Jock Stein	Halmstad
Roy Hodgson	Degerfors

Answers on page 112.

You want Messi? Not for all the Ice Cream in Manchester!

Anyone who's read our Xmas Football book, will know there have been some very strange transfer fees … a barrel of beer, a man's bodyweight in prawns … want to hear more?

How about **Hughie McLenahan**? – sold by Stockport to Manchester United for a freezer full of Ice cream. Then we have **Zat Knight** – he arrived at Fulham on a free from non-league Rushall Olympic. Fulham's owner felt that 'free' was a bit too much of a bargain, so gave Rushall 30 tracksuits. And finally, **Angus Morrison** moved from Ross County to Derby for a box of cigars! He scored almost a goal every other game at Derby, so we hope they were good cigars.

Now we're pretty sure those stories are true, but we also read that **Collins John**, a Dutch international who played for Fulham (and about a dozen other teams) was transferred to his first club for a set of dictionaries. We really want to believe this, but find it a little convenient that one of the most common dictionaries you can buy is made by … 'Collins'. It reminds us of a quote from **Tony Cascarino**. When asked if the rumours were true that he was once transferred for a set of tracksuits and some corrugated iron, Tony said, "It's one of those stories, it's just been exaggerated over time, going from ten tracksuits to a few cones, and all the rest. It's like the two loaves and five fishes in the Bible." So there, you have it – Tony Cascarino probably wasn't ever transferred for a corrugated iron fee.

QUIZ 9 - This is Definitely, Hopefully, Possibly Our Year!

1. Who were the first World Cup hosts to fail to get past the group stage?

2. Which team is also known as the Hornets?

3. Which Liverpool manager probably regrets saying, "You can't say my team aren't winners. They've proved that by finishing fourth, third and second in the last three years"?

4. Leicester City won their first ever Champions League tie 3-0, away from home. Which team did they beat?

5. Which club played home games at Spotland?

6. How many times was David Beckham voted the PFA Players' Player of the Year?

7. Which team won the very first Welsh League title in 1904/05? Rogerstone, Aberdare or Cwmaman?

8. In the seven seasons between 1959 and 1965, one player was the top scorer in the First Division on no less than five occasions. Who was he?

9. Who won the FA Cup in 2011?

10. Which player, who later captained Manchester City to their first Women's Super League title, was top scorer for Great

Britain at the 2012 Olympics? Steph Houghton, Kelly Smith or Jill Scott?

See page 88 for the answers.

Unusual Injuries: The Power Drill

#3 Darius Vassell

Darius Vassell – Speedy, skilful, and scorer of half a dozen goals for England. One day, Darius had a blood blister under his toe-nail, so he used his power drill to make a hole in the nail and release the blood.

It worked - unfortunately he got a blood infection instead.

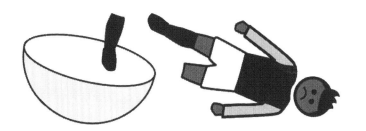

Quiz 10 – The Business End of the Season

1. Following the 1998 World Cup final there were plenty of conspiracy theories about why Brazil lost. Who cleared things up by saying, "We lost because we didn't win"?

2. Which club played home games at the Alexandra Stadium?

3. We all recognise the UEFA Champions League anthem, but do you know its official title?

4. In what year did Wales first qualify for the World Cup?

5. Who won the FA Cup in 1994?

6. Who was the first England player to be sent off at a World Cup finals?

7. Which team won the Premier League title in the 2004/05 season?

8. Who won the PFA Players' Player of the Year in 2005?

9. By what nickname are Portsmouth known?

10. Which Italian midfield genius wrote about his life in the book *I think therefore I play*?

See page 90 for the answers.

Name the Team #6

NEVER-1
+
1,000,000g
=

Find the answer at the bottom of the next page.

Everyone's gotta earn a livin'

If you're old enough to remember the days before the Premier League (when players had to save up if they wanted to buy a Lamborghini), you'll know that footballers had to get proper jobs once they retired. There weren't enough seats in the Match of the Day studio for everyone, so they ran pubs instead. Ok, not all of them, some of them did things differently, and there are even players today who have jobs. Even though they're rich enough to sit at home and play FIFA all day, they still want to work! So read on ...

Neil Webb played more than two dozen times for England, scored in (and won) a League Cup final for Nottingham Forest, helped Man United win the European Cup Winners' Cup, and delivered letters, parcels, and junk mail in the Reading postcode area. We don't know whether Postman Neil has a black and white cat, but we do like to imagine that just once in a while he flicks up a parcel with his right foot, taps it over the gate with his left, and heads it onto the doorstep of an unsuspecting Reading resident.

John Chiedozie played international football for Nigeria, and in 1981 Notts County paid £600k for his services. The first million pound transfer took place just two years earlier, so we reckon that's over £20 million in new money. So, what did he do after retiring? Well, if you're a kid in Hampshire, and you want to bounce up and down on an inflatable castle, John is the guy you call (just to be clear, he ran a business renting soft play / bouncy castles. He doesn't just have a bouncy castle in his garden that's free to use for local kids).

Dutch defender **Arjan De Zeeuw** played over 500 games in England, but now, if you check his pockets, you won't find a Premier league attacker, but a Dutch police warrant card. Dealing with cases ranging from burglary to human trafficking, and with an interest in crime scene investigations, this one may sound like the plot of a new TV show, but for Arjan, it's real life.

Robbie Fowler scored over 250 goals in his career, and won numerous trophies with Liverpool, but for many people he's the man they call when the boiler breaks down, "The Landlord". He's done so well from his property investments that, while playing, he was often serenaded (to the tune of Yellow Submarine) with the song, "We all live in a Robbie Fowler house … a Robbie Fowler house … a Robbie Fowler house!"

Want more? How about …

Stuart Ripley – from Blackburn Rovers winger to solicitor.

Gaizka Mendieta – Middlesbrough midfield to Superstar DJ!

Jeff Whitley – Man City midfield to used car salesman in Stockport.

Ray Wilson – England World Cup Winner turned undertaker.

Dave Hillier – Title winner with Arsenal to fireman in Bristol.

The Worst Teams in the World

Brazil, Germany, Spain, blah, blah, blah! Some teams get all the attention … simply because they're "good" or "win games". Well we've had enough. Time for the teams lower down the FIFA rankings to fight back – by starring in their very own word search. Look up, down, sideways, diagonally and backwards.

```
P I M N T N H Q W S J Y S S S
S U T F A U G M Z Z E A O P D
G A J I X Q O O T Z I L U A N
F C N U H N Z Q E N O M K K A
B A B M G A U Z O M F F J I L
G M S O A E T D O P R M B S S
U T L H N R E N V N L U V T I
F I Q B F L I E X W V E K A N
A F T U A S P N K T E P N N A
N V X C L X V C O B Z A H F M
M Y W A M O N T S E R R A T Y
A E N I U G W E N A U P A P A
N D R Z P S H P Q E D I W L C
S S C P K A R R O D N A O J K
C K J W Q I I G Z A F S O V Q
```

ANDORRA, CAYMAN ISLANDS, MACAU, MONGOLIA, MONTSERRAT, NEW CALEDONIA, PAKISTAN, PAPUA NEW GUINEA, SANMARINO, SOLOMON ISLANDS, TAHITI

The solution is on page 118

Name the Team #7

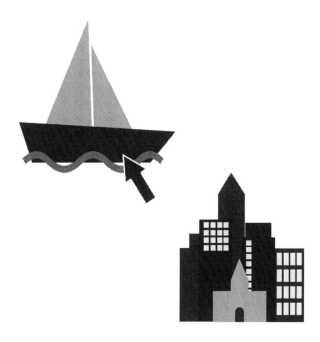

Find the answer at the bottom of the next page.

The Rules of the Game

The FA was formed in 1863, but football wasn't quite the same game as it is now …

Who needs refs?

A lot of players and fans would no doubt gladly get rid of refs, but can you imagine games without them? Originally it was assumed that players would always follow the rules, so there would be no disputes. That didn't last long. It was then up to the two captains to try and decide any contentious issues. That wasn't such a great idea either. 'Umpires' were next – but each team had their own, so not surprisingly arguments followed. A third official was finally added in 1881, the 'referee', who would be called upon when the two umpires disagreed.

It wasn't until nearly 20 years later that the ref was finally given control of the game on his own.

No Penalty!

Before the penalty kick was introduced (in 1891), defenders were punching the ball clear of the goal, or tripping an attacker as he was about to score, knowing that the punishment wouldn't be as severe as the crime. Once introduced, all such professional fouls disappeared overnight. And if you believe that …

Still there was at least one honourable tale following the introduction of the penalty. The Corinthians, a famous amateur team, played the game to the highest moral standards, and, if a penalty were awarded they would leave the goalmouth empty, allowing their opponents a free goal. They also apparently refused to score their own penalties, which seems a little too saintly if you ask us!

There's no substitute for subs

These days we hardly bat an eyelid when a grumpy manager takes off a player just because he didn't run about enough – but until the 1960s, subs weren't even allowed in English league football. This meant that if a player got injured, he'd usually try and play on. We've read of players with broken noses, jaws, ribs, and arms, playing through the pain. Bert Trautmann famously played for Man City, in the 1956 FA Cup Final, with five broken vertebrae in his neck!

Our favourite story, though, is of Alexander Fabian, a goalkeeper for Austrian club Hakoah Vienna in the 1920s. In the last game of the season, Fabian broke his arm. Hakoah were on course for the title, and couldn't risk losing the match, so Fabian was sent to play up front, with his arm in a sling! Within minutes he'd scored the winning goal, and the club won their first Austrian Championship.

Match the Celebrity to the Team

Apparently celebrities are real people too – and some of them like football! We know Ex-Prime Minister David Cameron is a fan of West Ham … I mean Aston Villa … (it's so easy to get the two mixed up), but can you match these stars to the clubs they support?

Gerard Butler	**Swansea City**
Hugh Grant	**West Ham United**
Kevin Costner	**Celtic**
Sylvester Stallone	**Rangers**
Gordon Ramsay	**Everton**
Daniel Craig	**Fulham**
Tom Hanks	**Liverpool**
Catherine Zeta-Jones	**Arsenal**
Keira Knightley	**Aston Villa**

See page 105 for the answers.

Quiz 11 – It's Semi-finals time!

1. Which team won the First Division title in the 1942/43 season?

2. Who was the top scorer at the 2002 World Cup Finals?

3. Who said amongst other things, "I'd love to be a mole on the wall in the dressing room", "You can't play with a one armed goalkeeper ... not at this level", "I know what is around the corner – I just don't know where the corner is" and "They're the second best team in the world, and there's no higher praise than that"?

4. Between 1982 and 1988, the English First Division title remained in the city of Liverpool. How many of those titles were won by Everton?

5. Where was the FA Cup final played in 2001?

6. By what nickname are Brentford known?

7. The curiously named Airbus UK Broughton were runners-up in which cup competition in 2016?

8. Which England, Stoke and Blackpool legend won the very first Ballon d'Or in 1956?

9. Which team won the Premier League title in the 2011/12 season?

10. Teams from Scotland won the European Cup in 1967, and the Cup Winners' Cup in 1972 and 1983. One man stands apart from all the players, subs and managers of those three cup winning teams. His name is Gerry Neef, and why was he different?

See page 92 for the answers.

Big Money transfers!
What would you do?

#3 Zlatan Ibrahimović

Instead of buying Zlatan Ibrahimović, Barcelona could have bought 13,563,218kg of IKEA meatballs.

We have nothing more to say.

Name the Team #8

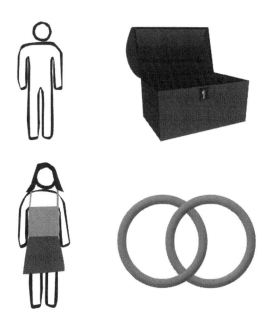

Find the answer at the bottom of the next page.

The Football League – Day Zero

The very first Football League season took place in 1888/89, and featured twelve clubs. The league was won by Preston North End, but all the competing teams are hidden in the word search below.

```
N P B R C E Y J Y Y U S B E H
N O I U K Z N H Z B A K E V S
V U T O R N G N Y R L V Q E C
M Q T G H N C R N E L Q O R U
N S O N N V L R X D I K P T A
A S U D N I U E M V V F A O Y
W Y E J Q B R Y Y R N L R N A
V F D V K U P C A R O P F F B
R J Y C L R O R C H T E W T P
M O A C G O Q K Z A S I J R N
X L E D L O W A J T A Z E E C
B N O T L O B D O O T S Y U D
K A T A W Q C W E S T B R O M
Y T N U O C S T T O N L K W I
H M Y E Q A E K N P L V O S O
```

ACCRINGTON, ASTON VILLA, BLACKBURN, BOLTON, BURNLEY, DERBY, EVERTON, NOTTS COUNTY, PRESTON, STOKE, WEST BROM, WOLVES

You can find the solution on page 106.

QUIZ 12 - Final Day Drama

1. In what year was the FA Cup final first played at Wembley Stadium?

2. 'Keep Right On' is sung by the fans of which Midlands based club?

3. Which footballer wrote about his life in the book *Addicted*?

4. In the 1905/06 Northern Ireland league, Cliftonville and Distillery were tied at the end of the season. At the time, ties were decided with a play-off match. What was the unusual outcome?

5. How many times was Alan Shearer voted the PFA Players' Player of the Year?

6. Which team won the First Division title in the 1960/61 season?

7. Who are the Tractor Boys?

8. Almost all of the first 20 FA Cup finals were played at a cricket ground. Which one?

9. Which English player won the Golden Shoe, for being top scorer at the 1986 World Cup?

10. Luis Suárez took a bite out of an opponent at the 2014 World Cup Finals. Which player did he decide to nibble on?

See page 94 for the answers.

Mixed up Players – Anagrams #3

We've mixed up the letters in the names of some of the world's greatest players (and some who might not be so great)! Can you work them out?

1. Lone Missile

2. Annoy Eye Row

3. Arena Lasher

4. A Rigorous Gee

5. No Jury Chaff

6. I Am Chintz Viola Bar

7. And He Razed

8. Sorely Barks

9. A Sage Coupling

You can find the answers on page 116.

Name the Team #9

Find the answer at the bottom of the next page.

Match the Team to the Stadium

Draw a line between the team and their stadium.

New York Stadium   Sheffield United

The Shay   Barnsley

The Hawthorns   Blackpool

Deepdale   Bury

Fratton Park   Halifax Town

Bloomfield Road   Portsmouth

Oakwell   Preston North End

Gigg Lane   West Bromwich Albion

Bramall Lane   Rotherham United

See page 109 for the answers.

Name the Team #9: Southampton (South Ham Tonne)

It's my club and I'll do what I want!

Burner Phone

Ken Richardson, of Doncaster Rovers, paid two local criminals to burn down his club's stadium! Why? So he could claim the insurance and then sell the land to developers. Unfortunately, his penny pinching ways meant he didn't go for the highest class of criminal, and one of the arsonists left his mobile phone at the scene of the crime. Richardson was sent to prison for four years.

Don't eat the salad!

Maurizio Zamparini at Palermo took over the club in 2002. Since then they've had 37 managers. That's about one sacking every four and a half months, and would be enough to get you into any list of bizarre owners. The fact that he once said of his team's players, "I will cut off their testicles and eat them in my salad", and suggested that "We should put all of the referees in prison", is really just the icing on the bonkers cake.

That's not what crutches are for ...

Zdravko Mamic is obviously a follower of the fairly controversial 'management by violence' leadership style, judging by the number of people he's punched while working for Dinamo Zagreb. He attacked a member of the Croatian FA, a Dinamo director, an NK Zagreb player, and even a policeman. He even attacked a Zagreb city official, while on crutches, following an operation. It didn't slow him down – he just used them to hit the poor man!

Missing Consonants

Some of the greatest players who've ever lived. But can you identify them from just the vowels in their names?

1. _ e _ e

2. _ a _ a _ o _ a

3. _ i _ e _ i _ e   _ i _ a _ e

4. _ a _ i

5. _ o _ a _ _ i _ _ o

6. _ a _ i o   _ a _ _ a _ a _ o

7. _ e o _ _ e   _ e a _

8. _ i a _ _ u i _ i   _ u _ _ o _

9. _ a _ _   _ i _ e _ e _

10. _ o _ a _ _   _ _ u _ _ _

Answers on page 113.

Who's the real Player?

Think you can tell a real player from one we've just hilariously made up? Well, time to put your pride to the test. Which player is real? Which is fake?

1. Ed de Ball or Mark de Man?

2. Peter Pander or Dickie Whittington?

3. Danny Invincible or Mike Unbeatable?

4. Fleetwood Macintosh Marou or Creedence Clearwater Couto?

5. Norman Conquest or Roman Invasion?

6. Colin Bangs or Chico Explosao?

7. Freddie Fantastic or Felix Brilliant?

8. Roberto Dinamite or Ricardo Semtex?

9. Jean-Pierre Scorre-Scorre or Jean-Jacques Misse-Misse?

10. Roberto Bionico or Ricardo Automatico?

See page 119 for the answers.

QUIZ 13 - The Play-Offs

1. Which French footballer had a cameo in the live action Asterix film, *Asterix at the Olympic Games*?

2. Which club played home games at Pride Park Stadium?

3. French player Just Fontaine was top scorer at the 1958 World Cup. His record still stands, and doesn't look like being beaten any time soon. How many goals did he score? 12, 13 or 16?

4. Which team have won Northern Ireland's top division more times than anyone else?

5. Which English player scored a goal after just 27 seconds of their first match at the 1982 World Cup?

6. Which player, who began his senior career at Man United, was awarded "Best Young Player" at the 2014 World Cup?

7. "We didn't underestimate them. They were just a lot better than we thought." Impeccable logic from which England manager?

8. Who were the first Welsh team to win the FA Cup?

9. By what tasty nickname are Everton known?

10. Which British team was the first to win the European Cup?

See page 96 for the answers.

Name the Trophy #3

More trophy silhouettes – In a worrying twist, these are the actual trophies painted with some kind of black tar! That's going to be a pain to clean off … but in the meantime, can you name the Football trophies from around the world?

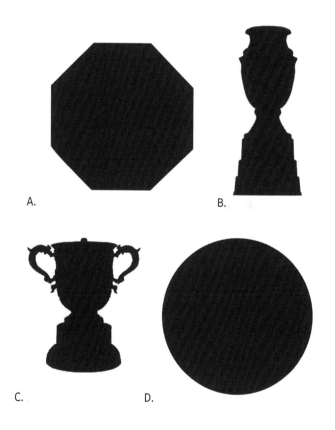

A.

B.

C.

D.

Answers on page 117.

Unusual Injuries:
The Corner Flag

#4 Thierry Henry

Thierry Henry scored more than 350 goals in his career. He played over 100 times for France. He won the World Cup. He won the Euros. He won the Champions League. He also managed to injure himself on a corner flag.

Apparently Thierry required treatment after hitting himself in the face with the flag, while celebrating a goal against Chelsea in 2000. Now, we can't find any pictures, and the reports are a bit flimsy too, but it was the winning goal, and well worth checking out on YouTube, so we don't think he'll mind us telling this story too much.

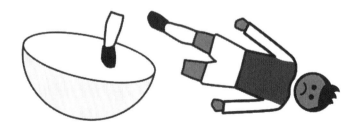

It's a Funny Old Game!

That was a definite penalty! We've been robbed!

Every football fan knows the feeling, but it's probably only Rotherham fans who literally have been robbed of a penalty. On Boxing Day, 2002, two fans of rival clubs, (Leeds and Sheffield United), broke into Rotherham's ground and stole the penalty spots. They planned to embed them in their own gardens, but the police, acting on a tip off from a Rotherham fan, caught them before they could plant their plunder. The two had to pay back £615 – the surprisingly expensive cost of replacing the spots.

Call the Physio! He's out cold!

When the United States played Argentina in the 1930 World Cup Semi-Finals, one of the US trainers overstepped the mark, resulting in a rather quick comeuppance. He ran onto the pitch to argue with the referee, throwing his medicine bag to the ground as he did so. A bottle of chloroform fell out, the top came off, and he was quickly knocked out by the fumes.

The ten minute manager

That might sound like the name of a book for all budding office managers, but for Leroy Rosenior it was a sad reality. He'd been manager of Torquay for four years when he left the club in January 2006. But, less than 18 months later, he was re-appointed. Unfortunately the job offer coincided with a club takeover, and the new owners promptly sacked him, after just 10 minutes in the job.

Big Money transfers!
What would you do?

#5 Paul Pogba

Manchester United fans could have been given twenty-five million, four hundred and twenty-eight thousand, five hundred and seventy-one free pies at Old Trafford.

Instead they got Paul Pogba. Let's hope he's worth it, as that's a whole lotta pie.

This was, of course, the second time that United had bought Pogba. The details of the first purchase were confidential, although as a sixteen-year-old we suspect it was for slightly less. What we do know is that when he left United to join Juventus, it wasn't even for the price of a single pie. Not a United Pie (whatever that is), a Steak Pie, or even a humble Meat & Potato Pie.

Name the Team #10

Find the answer at the bottom of the next page.

QUIZ 14 - The Cup Final

1. "Blue moon you saw me standing alone". What's the second line of the song that Man City fans sing?

2. Which ex-Liverpool, Villa and England striker appeared in *Basic Instinct 2*, with Sharon Stone?

3. Which South American team won the very first FIFA Fair Play trophy at a World Cup Finals? Columbia, Peru or Uruguay?

4. Who won the League Cup in 2013?

5. In what year did David Platt win the PFA Players' Player of the Year award?

6. Which south coast team won the last FA Cup final before the cup was suspended due to the Second World War?

7. *Snatch, Swordfish, Mean Machine, X-Men: The Last Stand.* Which ex-player connects these four films?

8. Which tyre company began sponsoring the English Women's League Cup in 2011?

9. By what nickname are Sheffield United known?

10. Only one player from Northern Ireland has ever won the Ballon d'Or. Can you name him, and the year he won?

See page 98 for the answers.

Name the Team #10: Bournemouth (Born Mouth)

Full Time!
Here are the
Answers!

QUIZ 1 – Back in Training

1. Which club's fans sing *Delilah*, the song made famous by Tom Jones?
   ANSWER: *Stoke City.*

2. The always entertaining ex-Manchester United star Eric Cantona played himself in which Ken Loach film?
   ANSWER: *Looking for Eric.*

3. Which team won the very first European Cup?
   ANSWER: *Real Madrid - they beat French club Reims in the final, 4-3. They also went on to win in each of the next four years!*

4. Which eccentric manager said, after winning a match, "I couldn't be more chuffed if I were a badger at the start of the mating season"?
   ANSWER: *Ian Holloway. And it's probably not even the funniest thing he said that week!*

5. Which team won the FA Cup an impressive four seasons in a row in the 1880s? Bury, Bolton or Blackburn Rovers?
   ANSWER: *Blackburn Rovers.*

6. Three players were sent off at the 1978 World Cup Finals. Two were from which East European country?

   ANSWER: *Hungary. The only other player to receive a red card was Dick Nanninga of the Netherlands. He was sent off for laughing when he was given a yellow card.*

7. Whose autobiography was called *Crossing the Line*?

   ANSWER: *Luis Suárez.*

8. Which West Midlands club won the very first English League Cup in 1961?

   ANSWER: *Aston Villa. The cup was played over two legs for the first six years, and in 1961 Villa beat Rotherham United 3-2 on aggregate.*

9. Manchester United won the first Premier League title, but which team won the final First Division title the previous year?

   ANSWER: *Leeds United in 1992.*

10. Which team is also known as the Addicks?

    ANSWER: *Charlton Athletic. Possibly because they served (H)addock at a local fish and chip shop!*

QUIZ 2 – Pre-Season Friendlies

1. English clubs won the European Cup every year between 1977 and 1982. Can you name the teams who won during that period? Double points if you get the order right!

   ANSWER: *Liverpool in 1977 and 78. Notts Forest in 79 and 80. Liverpool again in 81, and finally Aston Villa in 82.*

2. Which team is also known as the Baggies?

   ANSWER: *West Bromwich Albion. Definitely nothing to do with their kit's resemblance to Tesco Bags.*

3. Only one Leicester City player scored a league hat-trick during their 2015/16 title winning campaign? Name that player.

   ANSWER: *It was Riyad Mahrez, against Swansea City in December 2015.*

4. Which club, who play their home matches at Gigg Lane, won the first FA Cup of the 20th Century?

   ANSWER: *Bury.*

5. Which club played home games at the Britannia Stadium?

   ANSWER: *Stoke City.*

6. Which European country was the first to host a World Cup?

   ANSWER: *Italy. They beat Czechoslovakia in the final to win the whole competition.*

7. Which ex-England manager once said, "I was just saying to your colleague, the referee has got me the sack, thank him ever so much for that, won't you?"

    ANSWER: *Graham 'do I not like that' Taylor.*

8. Which London based team won the first three English Women's League Cup finals?

    ANSWER: *Arsenal - they reached the final the first times the competition was played, only losing once, to Manchester City, in 2014.*

9. In what year did Luis Suárez win the Ballon d'Or?

    ANSWER: *1960. If you got this one right, give yourself a pat on the back! The original Luis Suárez was a Spanish international who played in Italy for most of his career.*

10. By what name are the fans of the Scottish national team widely known?

    ANSWER: *The Tartan Army.*

QUIZ 3 – The Season Kicks Off

1. Which country's teams have won the UEFA Women's Champions League (also known as the UEFA Women's Cup) more than any other?

    ANSWER: *Germany. At the time this book was published, they'd won more than every other country put together!*

2. Whose autobiography was called *Full Time*?

    ANSWER: *Tony Cascarino. In the book he claimed to have been ineligible to play for Ireland despite being their record caps holder for a while. The Irish FA pointed out that he was eligible, and that he'd been feeling guilty all those years for no reason.*

3. 'Blue is the colour' is sung by fans of which Premier League club?

    ANSWER: *Chelsea.*

4. Which manager said, "I wouldn't say I was the best manager in the business, but I was in the top one"?

    ANSWER: *It was of course Brian Clough, and we'd probably have to agree.*

5. Which team is also known as the Bantams?

    ANSWER: *Bradford City.*

6. In 2002, two countries hosted the World Cup Finals for the first time. Can you name them?

   ANSWER: *South Korea and Japan were the joint hosts. South Korea even reached the semi-finals - although I wouldn't bring that up in Italy as they felt their team were robbed in a match against the hosts. Curiously, the referee was later suspended twice for making mistakes, and after his retirement became a drug smuggler.*

7. Who were the first sponsors of the Premier League?

   ANSWER: *Carling. Ironically, the 1990s was the decade when top players stopped drinking quite so many beers after games.*

8. Kevin Keegan is the only English player to have won more than one Ballon d'Or. He won both times while playing for the same team - can you name the club?

   ANSWER: *Hamburg. Keegan played in Germany for three seasons in the late 1970s*

9. In which decade did Aston Villa win their first FA Cup?

   ANSWER: *The 1880s. They first won in 1887, beating West Brom in the final.*

10. Which club played home games at the King Power Stadium?

    ANSWER: *Leicester City.*

QUIZ 4 – The First Round of The Cup

1. Who won the PFA Players' Player of the Year in 1994?
    ANSWER: *Eric Cantona.*

2. Who hosted the first World Cup Finals in 1930?
    ANSWER: *Uruguay. They also won the competition, at which 13 countries were represented. Yes, I did say 13 - work that one out!?*

3. Which club played home games at Vicarage Road?
    ANSWER: *Watford.*

4. Which club's fans sing 'I'm Forever Blowing Bubbles'?
    ANSWER: *West Ham United.*

5. In 2003, Milan beat Juventus to win the European Cup at which English team's ground?
    ANSWER: *The match was played at Manchester United's stadium, Old Trafford.*

6. We've all heard of Match of the Day, but from 2001-2004 the BBC lost the rights to broadcast Premier League highlights to ITV. What was ITV's highlights show called?
    ANSWER: *The Premiership. It was presented by Des Lynam, who had presented Match of the Day for the BBC until 1999.*

7. Which Scottish team won the 1983 European Cup Winners' Cup?

    ANSWER: *Aberdeen. They beat some unknowns called Real Madrid in the final (2-1 after extra time).*

8. Which manager (who had a pretty impressive career as a player too) called his autobiography *Walking on Water*?

    ANSWER: *Brian Clough.*

9. Which sister and brother have represented the English and Nigerian national teams, respectively?

    ANSWER: *Eni and Sone Aluko. Ironically, Eni played for England, but was born in Nigeria, while Sone was born in England but plays for Nigeria.*

10. Which manager said, "Mind you, I've been here during the bad times too - one year we came second"?

    ANSWER: *Bob Paisley of Liverpool (when they were winning just about everything).*

QUIZ 5 – The Early Leaders

1. In 1986, Steaua Bucharest became the first Eastern European club to win the European Cup. Where are they from?
   ANSWER: *Romania.*

2. In 2010, the 'Europe only' Ballon d'Or combined with FIFA's World Player of the Year to become an award for the best player anywhere in the world. Who won that 2010 award?
   ANSWER: *Lionel Messi. Despite now being a 'worldwide' award, it continues to be dominated by players in Europe.*

3. Who coined the phrase "squeaky-bum time" - for when the season is nearing its denouement?
   ANSWER: *Alex Ferguson. And yes, we did just use a French word.*

4. Arsenal won the UEFA Women's Cup in 2006/07. In the final, they beat a team from which country?
   ANSWER: *Arsenal beat Umeå IK of Sweden 1-0 on aggregate over a two-legged final.*

5. Which ex-Premier League player turned TV Pundit called his biography *Killa*?
   ANSWER: *It was Kevin Kilbane. We like Kevin, but we suspect his book is a little less exciting than the title.*

6. Which team is also known as the Black Cats?
   ANSWER: *Sunderland.*

7. The ground is the Liberty Stadium but who are the team?
   ANSWER: *Swansea City.*

8. Which brand were the very first sponsors of the English Football League?
   ANSWER: *Canon.*

9. "Glory Glory ..." - if we sang the rest, you'd know the answer. Which club's song is this?
   ANSWER: *Manchester United*

10. Who won the FA Cup in 1971?
    ANSWER: *Arsenal. They beat Liverpool 2-1.*

QUIZ 6 – The Local Derby

1. Who won the World Cup final in 2006?
   ANSWER: *Italy. They beat France on penalties.*

2. The ground is Brunton Park but who are the team?
   ANSWER: *Carlisle United.*

3. Which whisky brand were the first sponsor of the Scottish League Cup?
   ANSWER: *Bell's.*

4. Everton run onto the pitch to the theme from which 1960s TV police show?
   ANSWER: *Z-Cars. Why they do this, we don't know. Perhaps you could ask them?*

5. In what year did Luis Suarez win the PFA Players' Player of the Year award?
   ANSWER: *2014.*

6. Which club have won the European Cup and its successor, The Champions League, the most times?
   ANSWER: *Real Madrid.*

7. Whose autobiography is called *My Turn*?
   ANSWER: *Johann Cruyff. It's because of his Cruyff Turn, you know. And probably has some other meaning that makes it really clever.*

8. Who won the FA Cup in 1981?

    ANSWER: *Tottenham Hotspur. They beat Man City 3-2 in a replay, with Ricky Villa scoring a pretty good goal.*

9. 2015/16 was the first time Leicester City had won England's top division. They joined an exclusive club of only five 'one-time winners' - can you name the other four?

    ANSWER: *Sheffield United were the first in 1887/8, followed by West Bromwich Albion in 1919/20. Ipswich Town won the title for the only time in 1961/62 and finally Nottingham Forest won the 1977/78 title.*

10. Who was the first player to reach 150 caps for the England Women's team?

    ANSWER: *Fara Williams. At the time of writing, she is the most capped player in the history of English football.*

QUIZ 7 – The Busy Xmas Period

1. Who won the FA Cup in 1984?
   ANSWER: *Everton.*

2. The 1970 World Cup finals were hosted by Mexico, but which country won the competition?
   ANSWER: *Brazil. This was their third win.*

3. Which London club are known as the Hoops?
   ANSWER: *Queens Park Rangers - because their kit is stripey.*

4. How many times was Gareth Bale voted the PFA Players' Player of the Year?
   ANSWER: *Twice.*

5. Which manager said of his club's fans, "If you eat caviar every day it's difficult to return to sausages"?
   ANSWER: *Arsène Wenger, when the fans booed after a home draw with Middlesbrough.*

6. When Celtic were beaten by Inverness Caledonian Thistle, in February 2000, what was the famous headline in the next day's paper?
   ANSWER: *"Super Caley go ballistic, Celtic are atrocious".*

7. Which ex-player wrote the book *How Not to Be a Professional Footballer?*

    ANSWER: *Paul Merson. Another player who liked booze and betting a little too much - but he certainly knew how to kick a ball!*

8. Which team is also known as the Canaries?

    ANSWER: *Norwich City. We read this was due to the popularity of canary breeding in Norfolk - but really? Canary breeding? Really?! Canaries?! breeding?!*

9. One of England's most successful women's teams was founded in 1969 by lottery ticket sellers at the Belle View stadium. In which town were the 'Belles' based?

    ANSWER: *Doncaster. They later became Doncaster Rovers Belles Ladies Football Club, because your name can never be too long, apparently.*

10. The ground is Ashton Gate Stadium but who are the team?

    ANSWER: *Bristol City.*

QUIZ 8 – Mid-Season Madness

1. Who won the Scottish Football League Premier Division in the 1982/83 season?
   ANSWER: *Dundee United. At the time, Rangers had won the title 37 times, and Celtic 33. This was Dundee United's first win.*

2. Who won the World Cup final in 1982?
   ANSWER: *Italy beat West Germany 3-1.*

3. By what nickname are Stoke City known?
   ANSWER: *The Potters.*

4. How many times have the host country won the World Cup? If you can name them all, give yourself ten imaginary bonus points!
   ANSWER: *Six. Uruguay (1930), Italy (1934), England (1966), West Germany (1974), Argentina (1978) and France (1998).*

5. Which Midlands side won the English First Division title three times in the 1950s?
   ANSWER: *Wolverhampton Wanderers.*

6. Which London Women's Super League team did England winger Karen Carney sign for in December 2015?
   ANSWER: *Chelsea.*

7. Which English manager has won the European Cup / Champions League the most times?

   ANSWER: *Bob Paisley. He won three times with Liverpool.*

8. The ground is Roots Hall but who are the team?

   ANSWER: *Southend United.*

9. Which Italian manager, who never played top level football, said, "You don't have to have been a horse to be a jockey"?

   ANSWER: *Arrigo Sacchi. He didn't do too badly either, taking Italy to a World Cup final.*

10. Who won the FA Cup in 2008?

    ANSWER: *Portsmouth. They beat Cardiff 1-0.*

QUIZ 9 - This is Definitely, Hopefully, Possibly Our Year!

1. Who were the first World Cup hosts to fail to get past the group stage?
    ANSWER: *South Africa in 2010.*

2. Which team is also known as the Hornets?
    ANSWER: *Watford*

3. Which Liverpool manager probably regrets saying, "You can't say my team aren't winners. They've proved that by finishing fourth, third and second in the last three years"?
    ANSWER: *Gerard Houllier. Although to be fair, his English is better than my French.*

4. Leicester City won their first ever Champions League tie 3-0, away from home. Which team did they beat?
    ANSWER: *Club Brugge of Belgium.*

5. Which club played home games at Spotland?
    ANSWER: *Rochdale.*

6. How many times was David Beckham voted the PFA Players' Player of the Year?
    ANSWER: *None. Although he was twice runner-up in the FIFA World Player of the Year awards.*

7. Which team won the very first Welsh League title in 1904/05? Rogerstone, Aberdare or Cwmaman?

   ANSWER: Aberdare. And if you knew that without guessing then we're going to assume you're Welsh. In which case you need to know that Mae fy hofrenfad yn llawn llyswennod. Which we hope means 'My hovercraft is full of eels'.

8. In the seven seasons between 1959 and 1965, one player was the top scorer in the First Division on no less than five occasions. Who was he?

   ANSWER: Jimmy Greaves.

9. Who won the FA Cup in 2011?

   ANSWER: Manchester City - beating Stoke 1-0 in the final.

10. Which player, who later captained Manchester City to their first Women's Super League title, was top scorer for Great Britain at the 2012 Olympics? Steph Houghton, Kelly Smith or Jill Scott?

    ANSWER: Steph Houghton. She scored 3 goals as Great Britain progressed to the quarter-finals. The highlight was a winner against Brazil in front of over 70,000 fans at Wembley.

QUIZ 10 – The Business End of the Season

1. Following the 1998 World Cup final there were plenty of conspiracy theories about why Brazil lost. Who cleared things up by saying, "We lost because we didn't win"?
   ANSWER: *Ronaldo, who originally wasn't in the Brazil line up, apparently after being taken ill during the day. In the end he played, but not very well.*

2. Which club played home games at the Alexandra Stadium?
   ANSWER: *Crewe Alexandra. The stadium is also known as Gresty Road.*

3. We all recognise the UEFA Champions League anthem, but do you know its official title?
   ANSWER: *It's imaginatively titled 'Champions League'.*

4. In what year did Wales first qualify for the World Cup?
   ANSWER: *1958. They drew all their group matches, and had to play a second match against Hungary to decide who progressed. Wales won, but were then beaten 1-0 by Brazil, in the quarter-finals, with Pelé scoring his first ever international goal.*

5. Who won the FA Cup in 1994?
   ANSWER: *Manchester United beat Chelsea 4-0.*

6. Who was the first England player to be sent off at a World Cup finals?

   ANSWER: *Ray Wilkins, in a goalless draw with Morocco at the 1986 World Cup finals.*

7. Which team won the Premier League title in the 2004/05 season?

   ANSWER: *Chelsea.*

8. Who won the PFA Players' Player of the Year in 2005?

   ANSWER: *John Terry.*

9. By what nickname are Portsmouth known?

   ANSWER: *Pompey.*

10. Which Italian midfield genius wrote about his life in the book *I think therefore I play*?

    ANSWER: *Andrea Pirlo. It's a bit (ok - a lot) more philosophical than most footballers' autobiographies, but well worth reading.*

QUIZ 11 – It's Semi-finals time!

1. Which team won the First Division title in the 1942/43 season?

   ANSWER: *None. The league was suspended due to the Second World War.*

2. Who was the top scorer at the 2002 World Cup Finals?

   ANSWER: *Brazil's Ronaldo, who scored 8 goals.*

3. Who said amongst other things, "I'd love to be a mole on the wall in the dressing room", "You can't play with a one armed goalkeeper … not at this level", "I know what is around the corner – I just don't know where the corner is" and "They're the second best team in the world, and there's no higher praise than that"?

   ANSWER: *It was Kevin Keegan - truly the king of nonsense.*

4. Between 1982 and 1988, the English First Division title remained in the city of Liverpool. How many of those titles were won by Everton?

   ANSWER: *Two - in 1985 and 1987.*

5. Where was the FA Cup final played in 2001?

   ANSWER: *The Millennium Stadium in Cardiff. The cup was played there while Wembley was being rebuilt.*

6. By what nickname are Brentford known?

   ANSWER: *The Bees.*

7. The curiously named Airbus UK Broughton were runners-up in which cup competition in 2016?

   ANSWER: *They were beaten in the Welsh Cup final. The team who beat them are the answer to one of other quizzes, so we're not going to tell you who it was!*

8. Which England, Stoke and Blackpool legend won the very first Ballon d'Or in 1956?

   ANSWER: *Stanley Matthews. Matthews retired in 1965, at the ripe old age of 50. Amazingly, he was still playing in England's top division at the time!*

9. Which team won the Premier League title in the 2011/12 season?

   ANSWER: *Manchester City - although they did cut it fine, scoring twice against QPR in injury time to deny Manchester United on goal difference.*

10. Teams from Scotland won the European Cup in 1967, and the Cup Winners' Cup in 1972 and 1983. One man stands apart from all the players, subs and managers of those three cup winning teams. His name is Gerry Neef, and why was he different?

    ANSWER: *Every single player, sub and manager was Scottish, apart from Gerry, or Gerhard Neef, who was German.*

QUIZ 12 - Final Day Drama

1. In what year was the FA Cup final first played at Wembley Stadium?
   ANSWER: *1923. Bolton Wanderers beat West Ham United.*

2. 'Keep Right On' is sung by the fans of which Midlands based club?
   ANSWER: *Birmingham City*

3. Which footballer wrote about his life in the book *Addicted*?
   ANSWER: *Tony Adams.*

4. In the 1905/06 Northern Ireland league, Cliftonville and Distillery were tied at the end of the season. At the time, ties were decided with a play-off match. What was the unusual outcome in this season?
   ANSWER: *Play-offs have decided the league on eight other occasions, but this time the teams couldn't be separated, even after a second play-off, and for the only time in the league's history the title was shared.*

5. How many times was Alan Shearer voted the PFA Players' Player of the Year?
   ANSWER: *Twice.*

6. Which team won the First Division title in the 1960/61 season?
   ANSWER: *Tottenham Hotspur.*

7. Who are the Tractor Boys?

   ANSWER: *Ipswich Town.*

8. Almost all of the first 20 FA Cup finals were played at a cricket ground. Which one?

   ANSWER: *The Oval (also known as Kennington Oval).*

9. Which English player won the Golden Shoe, for being top scorer at the 1986 World Cup?

   ANSWER: *Gary Lineker. Not bad for a crisp salesman.*

10. Luis Suárez took a bite out of an opponent at the 2014 World Cup Finals. Which player did he decide to nibble on?

    ANSWER: *Italy's Giorgio Chiellini. This was the third time that Suárez had bitten an opponent. It's a tradition in football that if you do something three times you get to keep it. If you score a hat-trick, you take home the match ball. If you win the World Cup three times, you used to keep the trophy. We're not sure if Suárez got to keep a bit of Chiellini, and we're a bit scared to ask either player.*

QUIZ 13 – The Play-Offs

1. Which French footballer had a cameo in the live action Asterix film, *Asterix at the Olympic Games*?
    ANSWER: *It was Zinedine Zidane. Surely a highlight of his career.*

2. Which club played home games at Pride Park Stadium?
    ANSWER: *Derby County.*

3. The French player Just Fontaine was top scorer at the 1958 World Cup. His record still stands, and doesn't look like being beaten any time soon. How many goals did he score? 12, 13 or 16?
    ANSWER: *He scored 13 goals in just six games.*

4. Which team have won Northern Ireland's top division more times than anyone else?
    ANSWER: *Linfield. And we're not worried about this answer going out of date as they've won over 50 times, more than twice as many titles as any other club!*

5. Which English player scored a goal after just 27 seconds of their first match at the 1982 World Cup?
    ANSWER: *Bryan Robson, in a game where England beat France 3-1.*

6. Which player, who began his senior career at Manchester United, was awarded "Best Young Player" at the 2014 World Cup?

    ANSWER: *Paul Pogba.*

7. "We didn't underestimate them. They were just a lot better than we thought." Impeccable logic from which England manager?

    ANSWER: *Bobby Robson, following a match with Cameroon at the 1990 World Cup Finals.*

8. Who were the first Welsh team to win the FA Cup?

    ANSWER: *Cardiff. They beat Arsenal 1-0 in 1927. This was Cardiff's second final. They lost to Sheffield United two years earlier.*

9. By what tasty nickname are Everton known?

    ANSWER: *The Toffees, or Toffeemen.*

10. Which British team was the first to win the European Cup?

    ANSWER: *Celtic, in 1967.*

QUIZ 14 – The Cup Final

1. "Blue moon you saw me standing alone". What's the second line of the song that Man City fans sing?
   ANSWER: *Without a dream in my heart.*

2. Which ex-Liverpool, Villa and England striker appeared in *Basic Instinct 2*, with Sharon Stone?
   ANSWER: *Stan Collymore (p.s. don't try to watch this if you're under 18, or if you'd rather not have to wash your eyes out with soap afterwards!)*

3. Which South American team won the very first FIFA Fair Play trophy at a World Cup Finals? Columbia, Peru or Uruguay?
   ANSWER: *Peru.*

4. Who won the League Cup in 2013?
   ANSWER: *Swansea City.*

5. In what year did David Platt win the PFA Players' Player of the Year award?
   ANSWER: *1990.*

6. Which south coast team won the last FA Cup final before the cup was suspended due to the Second World War?
   ANSWER: *Portsmouth. They beat Wolves 4-1 in 1939.*

7. *Snatch, Swordfish, Mean Machine, X-Men: The Last Stand.* Which ex-player connects these four films?

    ANSWER: *It is of course Vinnie Jones, arguably the most successful ex-footballer turned movie star. It's probably fair to say his talents in both areas were limited, but he certainly made the most of them!*

8. Which tyre company began sponsoring the English Women's League Cup in 2011?

    ANSWER: *Continental.*

9. By what nickname are Sheffield United known?

    ANSWER: *The Blades. Sheffield was famous for steel, and steel knives have blades. Simple.*

10. Only one player from Northern Ireland has ever won the Ballon d'Or. Can you name him, and the year he won?

    ANSWER: *It was of course George Best. He won the award in 1968.*

Who's the player?

1. He was born on 25th April 1947, and is a three time winner of the Ballon D'or. He played in the United States, with the Los Angeles Aztecs and the Washington Diplomats, and went on to manage the Catalonia 'national' team. Name that player.
   ANSWER: *It was of course the great Johan Cruyff, slightly more famous for his associations with Ajax and Barcelona, and for his fancy 'turn'.*

2. Born on the 29th September 1976, he began and ended his professional career at Dynamo Kyiv. He also played over 100 times for his national team, scoring almost 50 goals. Who's the player?
   ANSWER: *The Ukrainian superstar Andriy Shevchenko. While he started and ended his career at Dynamo, he played for Milan and Chelsea in between.*

3. Born in Rosario on the 24th June 1987, he was a youth player with Newell's Old Boys, and later won an Olympic gold medal for his country. Who is he?
   ANSWER: *It's only Lionel Messi! He's done a few other things in his time, but we're not here to make things easy for you!*

4. She began her senior career with Vasco de Gama in Brazil, and was the FIFA World Player of the Year five times. Name the player?
   ANSWER: *Marta of Brazil. Considered by many to be the best female footballer of all time.*

5. Born in Chester on the 14th December 1979, this footballer ended his playing career with Stoke City. He also scored four goals for England at World Cup finals. Name the player.

    ANSWER: *Michael Owen. He only played a few games for Stoke, and is of course more famous for his time at Liverpool, Real Madrid, Newcastle and Man United.*

He can play a bit, that lad!
A Messi Spot the Difference!

Answers: Accent on letter á, Rounded/straight corners on header box, Different nose, Missing penalty spot on board, Extra X on board, White panel on ball, Different socks, Missing lace.

Name the Trophy #1

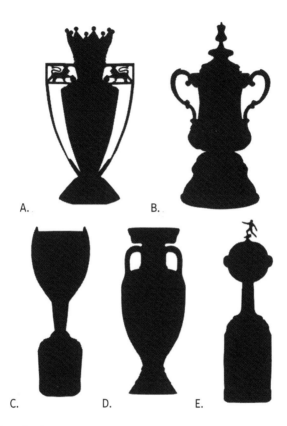

A.

B.

C. D. E.

A. Premier League

B. FA Cup

C. Jules Rimet (original World Cup)

D. Euros

E. Copa Libertadores

You Called Your Stadium What? #1

The real answers are in bold below! Hope you got them right – and I hope your team don't play at any of them!

1. Point of Sale Park or **Cashpoint Arena**?

2. **Hunky Dorys Park** or Okey Dokey Stadium?

3. **Tony Macaroni Arena** or Campo Carbonara?

4. Burger King Stadium or **Pizza Hut Park**?

5. The Lard Pan or **The Dripping Pan**?

6. **Middelfart Stadium** or Upperguff Arena?

7. Snickers Bay Park or **Kitkat Crescent**?

8. Cash Converters Arena or **Bargain Booze Stadium**?

Match the Celebrity
to the Team

Gerard Butler..Celtic

Hugh Grant... Fulham

Kevin Costner... Arsenal

Sylvester Stallone ....Everton

Gordon Ramsay.. Rangers

Daniel Craig...Liverpool

Tom Hanks... Aston Villa

Catherine Zeta-Jones.............................Swansea City

Keira Knightley................................ West Ham United

The Football League – Day Zero

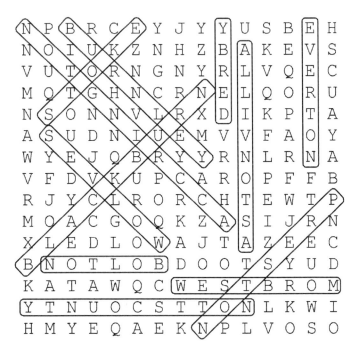

They started out where?

1. Joe Hart made his debut with Shrewsbury Town.

2. Dele Alli made his debut with Milton Keynes Dons.

3. Wayne Rooney made his debut with Everton.

4. Eric Dier made his debut with Sporting Lisbon (he first played for their B team - who play in the lower divisions in Portugal).

5. Gary Cahill made his debut with Aston Villa.

6. John Stones made his debut with Barnsley.

7. Daniel Sturridge made his debut with Manchester City.

8. Alex Oxlade-Chamberlain made his debut with Southampton.

9. Jordan Henderson made his debut with Sunderland.

10. Fraser Forster made his debut with Stockport County.

Anagrams #1 Answers - Mixed up Stadiums

1. Old Trafford (Man United)

2. Stadium of Light (Sunderland)

3. Goodison Park (Everton)

4. White Hart Lane (Spurs)

5. King Power Stadium (Leicester City)

6. Craven Cottage (Fulham)

7. Tannadice (Dundee United)

8. Ewood Park (Blackburn Rovers)

9. Carrow Road (Norwich City)

Match the Team to the Stadium

New York Stadium.........................Rotherham United

The Shay...Halifax Town

The Hawthorns ....West Bromwich Albion

Deepdale.. Preston North End

Fratton Park .... Portsmouth

Bloomfield Road...Blackpool

Oakwell.. Barnsley

Gigg Lane ....Bury

Bramall Lane......................................Sheffield United

Name the Trophy #2

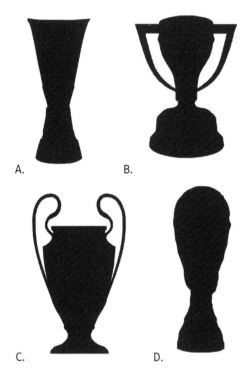

A.

B.

C.

D.

A. Europa League

B. La Liga

C. The Champions League

D. The World Cup

Anagrams #2 Answers - Mixed up Teams

1. Barcelona (Earl Bacon)

2. West Bromwich Albion (Bar Witch Snowmobile)

3. Wigan Athletic (A Twitching Ale)

4. Southampton (Phantoms Out)

5. Aston Villa (Vital Loans)

6. Newcastle United (I Select Unwanted)

7. Queens Park Rangers (Square Prank Genres)

8. Bury (Ruby)

9. Halifax Town (Lawn Fit Hoax)

Match the Manager to the Club

Bobby Robson.. Fulham

Alex Ferguson......................................East Stirlingshire

Fabio Capello ....Milan

Claudio Ranieri.........................Campania Puteolana

Brian Clough......................................Hartlepool United

Sven-Göran Eriksson......................................Degerfors

José Mourinho.. Benfica

Carlo Ancelotti...Reggiana

Jock Stein .... Dunfermline

Roy Hodgson ....Halmstad

Missing Consonants - Answers

1. Pele

2. Maradona

3. Zinedine Zidane

4. Xavi

5. Ronaldinho

6. Fabio Cannavaro

7. George Weah

8. Gianluigi Buffon

9. Gary Lineker

10. Johann Cruyff

Match the Club to the Country

Lincoln Red Imps .... Gibraltar

Pyunik .... Armenia

FC Santa Coloma ....Andorra

Folgore...San Marino

The New Saints.. Wales

Levadia Tallinn .... Estonia

B36 Tórshavn..Faroe Islands

Crusaders... Northern Ireland

Rudar Pljevlja... Montenegro

Stjarnan .... Iceland

1966 and All That!

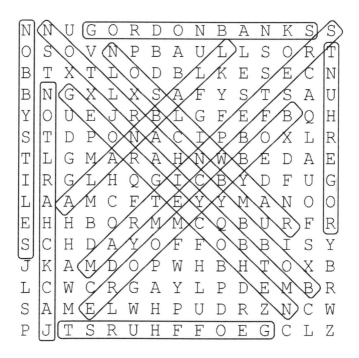

Anagrams #3 Answers - Mixed up Players

1. Lionel Messi (Lone Missile)

2. Wayne Rooney (Annoy Eye Row)

3. Alan Shearer (Arena Lasher)

4. Sergio Agüero (A Rigorous Gee)

5. Johan Cruyff (No Jury Chaff)

6. Zlatan Ibrahimović (I Am Chintz Viola Bar)

7. Eden Hazard (And He Razed)

8. Ross Barkley (Sorely Barks)

9. Paul Gascoigne (A Sage Coupling)

Name the Trophy #3

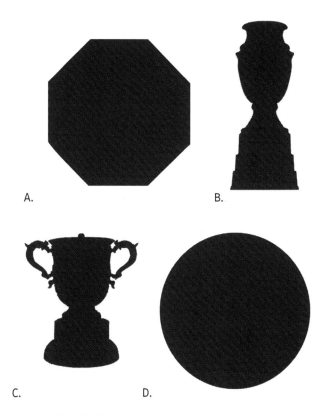

A.

B.

C.

D.

A. The Charity Shield

B. The Copa America

C. The Football League Cup

D. The Bundesliga (assuming no-one else has thought of "round")

The Worst Teams in the World

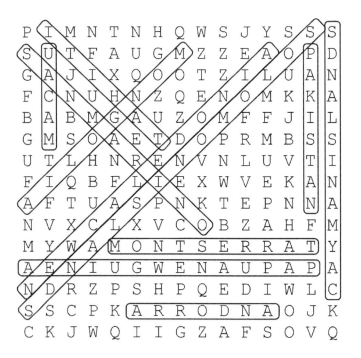

Who's the Real Player?

The real players are ...

1. Mark de Man. An aptly named Belgian footballer, born in 1983, who has spent most of his career with Anderlecht.

2. Peter Pander. Born in 1951, this German player was also sporting director of Borussia Mönchengladbach and Wolfsburg. Oh yes he was!

3. Danny Invincible. Danny is a well-travelled Australian who has played in Cyprus, Thailand, Scotland and er ...Swindon.

4. Creedence Clearwater Couto. Named after the rock band Creedence Clearwater Revival, this Brazilian's career failed to reach the same chart-topping heights.

5. Norman Conquest. Born in England in 1916, he later played international football for Australia.

6. Chico Explosao. Born in 1954, he played most of his career in his native Brazil.

7. Felix Brilliant. Born in 1980, Mr Brilliant has played in the US and Norway as well as in his home country, Canada.

8. Roberto Dinamite. The explosive Dinamite was a Brazilian international who scored his first goal for Brazil when they beat England in 1976.

9. Jean-Jacques Misse-Misse. He might be called Misse-Misse but he managed to score-score for teams in Belgium, Turkey, Greece and Cameroon.

10. Roberto Bionico. This Bionico man was a Brazilian journeyman playing for a range of clubs in his home country.